Date: 3/14/16

World's **WEIRDEST** Animals

Flying Squirrels

Big Buddy Books

An Imprint of Abdo Publishing
abdopublishing.com

Marcia Zappa

abdopublishing.com

Published by Abdo Publishing, a division of ABDO, PO Box 398166, Minneapolis, Minnesota 55439. Copyright © 2016 by Abdo Consulting Group, Inc. International copyrights reserved in all countries. No part of this book may be reproduced in any form without written permission from the publisher. Big Buddy Books™ is a trademark and logo of Abdo Publishing.

Printed in the United States of America, North Mankato, Minnesota.
042015
092015

Cover Photos: Nicholas Jr/Getty Images; Shutterstock.com.
Interior Photos: Arco Images GmbH Wothe, K./Glow Images (p. 29); Visuals Unlimited, Inc./Alexander Badyaev/Getty Images (p. 13); ©Biosphoto/AUSCAPE (p. 11); © Dick, Michael/Animals Animals-Earth Scenes (p. 19); ©iStockphoto.com (p. 30); Satoshi Kuribayashi/Nature Production/Minden Pictures (pp. 7, 21); © Lubeck, Robert/Animals Animals-Earth Scenes (p. 17); S & D & K Maslowski/FLPA/Minden Pictures (p. 27); Steve & Dave Maslowski (p. 23); Hiroji Motowaka/Nature Production/Minden Pictures (p. 9); Kim Taylor/npl/Minden Pictures (p. 5); ©Wild & Natural/Animals Animals-Earth Scenes (p. 25).

Coordinating Series Editor: Rochelle Baltzer
Contributing Editors: Megan M. Gunderson, Grace Hansen, Sarah Tieck
Graphic Design: Adam Craven

Library of Congress Cataloging-in-Publication Data

Zappa, Marcia, 1985- author.
 Flying squirrels / Marcia Zappa.
    pages cm. -- (World's weirdest animals)
 ISBN 978-1-62403-775-7
1. Flying squirrels--Juvenile literature. I. Title.
 QL737.R68Z37 2016
 599.36'9--dc23
                              2015004768

Contents

Wildly Weird!

The world is full of weird, wonderful animals. There are almost 50 different kinds of flying squirrels. These small, furry animals are known for **gliding** from tree to tree. This unusual skill makes flying squirrels wildly weird!

The longest glide ever recorded by a flying squirrel was about 1,500 feet (450 m). But, glides up to 150 feet (45 m) are more common.

Bold Bodies

Flying squirrels are **rodents**. Rodents are a type of **mammal**. Flying squirrels have soft fur. It may be gray, brown, black, or tan.

A flying squirrel's body and legs are long and thin. The animal's head has large ears and big, dark eyes. The tail may be long or short. It may be thin, fluffy, or flat.

EAR

EYE

BODY

LEG

TAIL

7

Different types of flying squirrels vary greatly in size. Some adults grow to be 24 inches (61 cm) long. Others are just 3 inches (8 cm) long. Adults weigh from 1 ounce (28 g) to 5.5 pounds (2.5 kg).

Did You Know?

The largest flying squirrel is the woolly flying squirrel. It lives in southern Asia.

Many types of giant flying squirrels are found in Asia. This includes the Japanese giant flying squirrel (*below*).

9

Great Gliders

Flying squirrels can't actually fly. But, they are excellent gliders.

A flying squirrel's body is built for gliding. Furry membranes connect each front leg to each back leg. Rods support the membranes. The rods are made of strong, but bendable tissue called cartilage (KAHR-tuh-lihj).

Did You Know?

A human's nose and ears are made of cartilage.

A flying squirrel moves its membranes and tail to change direction and speed in the air.

From high in a tree, a flying squirrel jumps into the air. It straightens out its legs. This stretches the **membranes** tight.

The flying squirrel uses its membranes like a **parachute** to **glide** gently downward. It lands on all four feet.

A flying squirrel uses its tail like a brake. The tail helps a squirrel slow down to land.

Where in the World?

Flying squirrels live in many places around the world. Most are found in Europe and Asia. Two types live in North America.

Flying squirrels make their homes in forests. Some live in **tropical** forests. Others are found in temperate forests. These have evergreen trees and trees that lose their leaves in the winter.

Europe

Asia

Africa

Indian Ocean

■ = **Flying Squirrel Region**

North America

N
W ✦ E
S

Pacific Ocean

South America

Australia

Did You Know?

The northern flying squirrel and the southern
flying squirrel live in North America.

Home Sweet Nest

Flying squirrels are nocturnal. That means they are active at night.

During the day, flying squirrels sleep in nests. These are often found in trees. They may be where branches come together or in holes in trunks. Nests are made of materials such as leaves, bark, and moss.

Did You Know?

Flying squirrels may also build nests in attics or birdhouses.

Sometimes, several flying squirrels share a nest to stay warm. This is common during the cold winter months in northern areas.

A Squirrel's Life

Most flying squirrels live almost entirely in trees. North American flying squirrels are found on the ground more regularly. There, they search for food and hide nuts to eat later.

When it isn't gliding, a flying squirrel keeps its membranes pulled in close to its body.

Flying squirrels have **predators** in the air, in trees, and on the ground. Owls, hawks, snakes, raccoons, and foxes hunt them. But, their special skill can often keep them safe. Flying squirrels escape danger by quickly **gliding** away!

After landing, a flying squirrel often runs to the other side of a large branch or tree trunk. This helps it escape any flying predators that may have been following it.

Favorite Foods

Flying squirrels are omnivores. That means they eat both plants and animals.

Flying squirrels eat a wide variety of foods. This includes seeds, nuts, fruits, leaves, bugs, and eggs. They may also eat small birds, other small animals, and dead animals. Their diet depends on where they live and what kind of squirrel they are.

Some flying squirrels in northern areas hide food such as nuts and seeds. They save it for the cold winter months when food is harder to find.

Life Cycle

Some types of flying squirrels **mate** twice a year. Others mate once a year. A few types may mate just once every 18 months.

Flying squirrel mothers give birth in their nests. They have up to seven babies at a time.

Newborn flying squirrels cannot see or hear. Most have bare skin.

Newborn flying squirrels drink their mother's milk and grow. Young flying squirrels grow quickly. After about two months, they are ready to leave the nest.

Did You Know?

Scientists are not sure how long flying squirrels live in the wild. They have lived more than ten years in zoos.

Sometimes, a mother needs to move her babies before they are ready to glide on their own. So, she carries them in her mouth.

World Wide Weird

Many types of flying squirrels are common. But, others are at risk. Much of their **habitat** has been cleared for lumber and to make room for buildings.

It is important to know how our actions affect wild animals. With care, we can keep weird, wonderful animals such as flying squirrels around for years to come.

Even though many types of flying squirrels are common, people don't see them often because they are nocturnal.

FAST FACTS ABOUT:
Flying Squirrels

Animal Type – mammal

Size – 3 to 24 inches (8 to 61 cm) long

Weight – 1 ounce (28 g) to 5.5 pounds (2.5 kg)

Habitat – forests in North America, Europe, and Asia

Diet – seeds, nuts, fruits, leaves, bugs, eggs, small birds, other small animals, and dead animals

What makes the flying squirrel wildly weird?

It uses stretched-out membranes on each side of its body to glide long distances between trees.

Glossary

glide to fall gradually without enough power for level flight.

habitat a place where a living thing is naturally found.

mammal a member of a group of living beings. Mammals make milk to feed their babies and usually have hair or fur on their skin.

mate to join as a couple in order to reproduce, or have babies.

membrane a thin, soft, bendable sheet of tissue that covers a part of an animal or plant.

parachute an umbrella-shaped piece of light fabric that is used for making a safe jump from an airplane.

predator a person or animal that hunts and kills animals for food.

rodent any of several related animals that have large front teeth for gnawing. Common rodents include mice, squirrels, and beavers.

tropical of or relating to parts of the world where temperatures are warm and the air is moist all the time.

Websites

To learn more about World's Weirdest Animals, visit **booklinks.abdopublishing.com**. These links are routinely monitored and updated to provide the most current information available.

Index